EXTRAORDINARY!



# THE BOOK OF ECO PAPER PROJECTS

Written by Susan Hayes and Penny Arlon
Illustrated by Pintachan

LOOK INSIDE FOR IDEAS ON HOW TO REUSE AND RECYCLE.

WINDMILL BOOKS

# A Message from Dr. Amy Dickman

## Conservationist and wildlife expert

Thank you for reading **The Extraordinary Book of Eco Paper Projects**! We live in such a beautiful world filled with incredible wildlife, from powerful lions to fascinating insects. We have rich forests, brilliant birds, amazing oceans and so much more – we are so lucky to call this planet our home.

Unfortunately, the world has problems, including too much waste. By using this book as inspiration to make environmentally friendly projects, you will have fun, avoid waste and help our amazing planet!

**Do you want to be good at reducing, reusing and recycling?**

On every page there are all sorts of interesting projects to make – from planters and seed writing papers to eco-badges.

There are eco-quizzes and nature games, growing projects and organic recipes, bug hotels and plastic-free gift bags.

There are many activities to do on your own, and others to try with an adult's help – all of which can help you to change the way you think about the natural world, and how you can make a real difference. And don't worry if what you do seems small. If everyone joins in with lots of small actions, together we can make a BIG difference!

Step by step **The Book of Eco Paper Projects** is your guide to taking action!

# CONTENTS

1

Design a wormery to compost food scraps.

# BUILD A WORMERY

## to recycle your food scraps

Instead of putting your food scraps into the landfill, send in the worms! Recycle in a green way.

The holes let the worms breathe.

The worms eat the leaves and peelings.

Release the worms after a couple of days.

Now talk to your family about making a bigger wormery. Composting ALL your scraps will make a difference.

### You will need

1/4 cup gravel

empty jar with lid

soil

1 tablespoon water

sand

leaves, vegetable peelings

earthworms

### Make a mini wormery

1 Put gravel into the bottom of a small, thin jar. Add a layer of soil and then sand.

2 Layer up more soil and sand. Drip a little water over the top.

3 Pop in three or four worms and a few leaves and vegetable scraps.

4 Ask an adult to make some holes in the jar lid. Screw it on.

5 Wrap a cover around your jar to keep it cool and dark.

Design a cover for your wormery to wrap around your jar. This will help keep it cool and dark. You can copy this picture or design one yourself.

2

# PASS AND SHARE

## to reduce buying and wasting

Share a bookmark with a friend

Invite friends to bring over a game, then swap.

Next time you are about to throw something away, think first. Who might use it? Swap books, toys and games with friends to avoid buying too many new things. Recycling is fun and helps to save the planet.

Grown out of your boots? Pass them on!

Pass a book on with a special bookmark inside.

Copy these designs onto 1.5 x 5 inch (4 cm x 13 cm) strips of card-stock.
Pop the bookmarks in books you would like to swap!

3

Can you take the plastic-free challenge?

# GO PLASTIC FREE

## to stop harming ocean creatures

Sadly, turtles often think plastic looks and smells like food, so they eat it.

Millions of tons of plastic are washed into oceans from rivers and beaches. Avoid plastic to keep our wildlife safe.

When a whale gulps water to catch fish, it catches plastic too, which blocks its gut.

### Five ways to avoid using plastic

Don't buy plastic bottles. Fill up a reusable one with water instead.

Take a reusable bag shopping to save buying a plastic one.

Say NO to plastic straws. Use a paper one or use no straw at all!

Ask your family to buy fruit and vegetables with no plastic packaging.

Pack a plastic-free lunch. Remember, no plastic wrap or plastic packets!

# Take the plastic-free challenge!

Copy this checklist to pin up at home.

| ✓ YES! | ✗ NO! |
| --- | --- |
| Bamboo toothbrush | Plastic toothbrush |
| Soap bar | Liquid soap in a plastic bottle |
| Loose vegetables | Plastic tub of vegetables |
| Reusable bag | Throw-away bag |
| Paper straw | Plastic straw |
| Reusable bottles | Plastic bottles |

You can make a difference and help the ocean creatures!

## WEEK 1 Plastic checklist

| Plastic item | How many in your home? |
| --- | --- |
| toothbrushes | ........................ |
| soap bottles | ........................ |
| bags | ........................ |
| straws | ........................ |
| tubs | ........................ |
| bottles | ........................ |

Count the plastic items. Can you make a difference?

## WEEK 4 Plastic checklist

| Plastic item | How many in your home? |
| --- | --- |
| toothbrushes | ........................ |
| soap bottles | ........................ |
| bags | ........................ |
| straws | ........................ |
| tubs | ........................ |
| bottles | ........................ |

Count again four weeks later. Did you make a difference?

# GROW YOUR OWN

## to save food miles

**4** Prepare home-grown strawberry treats.

Every day, fruit is taken from one place to another. This transportation releases harmful gases into the air.

**In most countries, strawberries are only in season for a few months a year. The rest come from abroad. Grow your own to help keep the air clean.**

Find out when is the best time to grow strawberries where you live.

### Grow a strawberry bag!

### You will need

strawberry plants

scissors

a canvas bag

compost

1 Ask an adult to snip holes in the bottom and sides of the bag. Add compost.

2 At each slit, pop in a plant, pushing the leaves out through the slits from inside.

3 Plant the final two plants in the top, covering the roots with soil. Water well.

4 Keep the bag in a sunny spot and water regularly.

# Strawberry Slushie

**You will need**

1 teaspoon sugar

3 ice cubes

juice of half a lemon

a sprig of mint

1 cup strawberries

1 With adult help, blitz the strawberries, ice cubes, lemon and sugar (optional) in a blender.

2 Serve in your favorite glass, and decorate with a sprig of mint!

# Strawberry Milkshake

**You will need**

2 cups strawberries

1 tablespoon honey (optional)

$1\frac{1}{2}$ cups milk

1 With adult help, put all the ingredients into a blender and blitz.

2 Pour into a glass and add a strawberry on top.

# Strawberries and Cream

**You will need**

strawberries

cream

sugar (optional)

1 Remove leaves and, with adult help, cut the berries in half.

2 Put them into a bowl and pour in the cream.

3 Sprinkle some sugar on top.

# Strawberry Ice Pop

**You will need**

$\frac{1}{2}$ cup strawberries

ice pop stick

1 teaspoon sugar

1 cup natural yogurt

1 With an adult, blitz ingredients in a blender.

2 Pour the mix into a reusable container. Pop a lolly stick in.

3 Freeze overnight. Take off the container and eat!

5

Design a cooling fan.

# TURN IT DOWN

## to save electricity

You don't always have to turn on the heating or air conditioning. There are other ways to stay warm or cool that don't waste electricity.

Have a warm drink to warm yourself up.

Add ice to a cold drink to help keep cool.

### Don't turn up the heat

1 Wear an extra thick sweater and socks instead.

2 Make sure you close windows to keep out draughts.

### Don't turn on the air conditioning

1 Keep blinds closed to block out the sun's heat.

2 Use a handmade fan to keep yourself cool.

Decorate a square of paper or card with a lovely picture. You can copy this one or use your own design.

## Make a cooling fan

1 Take your paper and fold one side over 1 inch (2.5 cm). Press firmly along the crease.

2 Turn over and fold the same amount on the other side.

3 Keep turning over and folding until you reach the end.

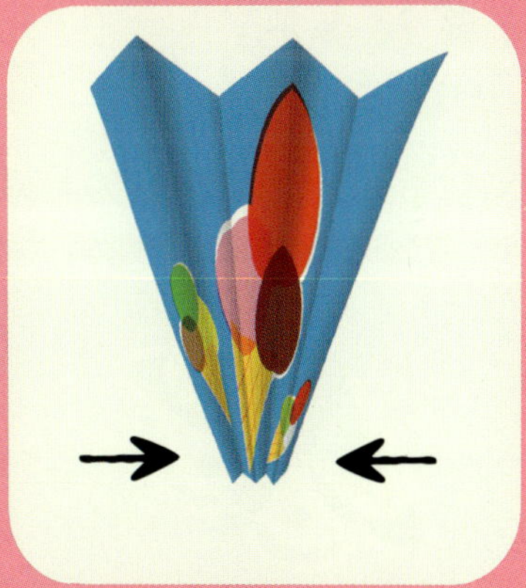

4 Squeeze one end together and fan yourself cool.

**6**

Save electricity by sending out reminders.

# TURN OFF THE LIGHTS

## to stop light pollution

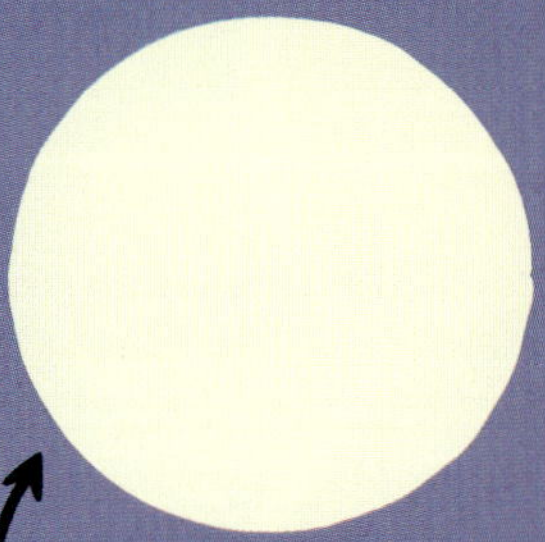

Lights glow above cities at night, lighting up the land. This confuses animals that need the darkness to keep safe.

Some animals use moonlight to find their way.

Most lights can be turned off at night.

### How city light affects animals

**Moths** use light from the moon to help find their way. They get confused and fly towards city lights instead.

**Tree frogs** call out in the dark to find a mate. Too much light means they don't call and don't breed.

**Voles** use darkness to hide from predators. City lights make them easier to spot.

**Turtles** use moonlight to find the sea from the beach when they hatch. Some head towards city lights instead.

Copy and pass on these messages to friends and family to remind them to turn their lights off at night.

To..........................................

Please remember to turn off lights at night.
Light pollution confuses animals.

To..................................

Light at night wastes electricity and is dangerous for animals. Please turn it off.

To..........................................

Save the animals! Help bring back darkness at night by turning your lights off.

To...............................................

Turn lights off to bring back dark nights.
It's safer for animals.

To.........................................

Stop light pollution and stop wasting electricity. Please turn off the lights at night.

# 7

Upcycle things you might have thrown away.

# UPCYCLE YOUR JUNK

## to reduce waste and save landfill space

### Turn something old into something new

1. Don't throw away your favorite old things. Use pictures and glue to upcycle.
2. Cut pictures from magazines or draw your own. Ideas are on the next page.
3. Ask an adult to help you make eco-friendly glue. Turn to project 30 for the recipe.
4. Use plenty of glue to stick the pictures onto your "treasure."
5. Paste more glue over the pictures to make them strong. Leave to dry overnight.

Copy these pictures onto paper and cut them out.

8

Send out eco-picnic invitations.

# HAVE AN ECO-PICNIC

## that doesn't harm the planet

1 Pick a local spot that you can walk or cycle to.

2 Pack a picnic with no plastic wraps.

3 Bring reusable drinks, bottles and cutlery.

4 Invite your friends. Remind them to be eco-friendly too.

5 Clean up and take your trash home.

Invite your friends to a picnic party!
Copy the invitation shown here or design your own.

**9**

Make garden markers.

# PLANT A TREE

## to help slow down climate change

If everyone on Earth planted just one tree, it would help climate change slow down.

Trees are amazing. They breathe in harmful carbon dioxide and turn it into oxygen.

Trees are also homes for wildlife.

Tree roots keep the soil stable, which helps to stop flooding.

### Plant a sapling

1 Put some gravel at the bottom of a pot. Fill it with soil.

2 Push a seed half a finger length into the soil. Water it so the soil is damp.

3 Keep the pot outside in a shady corner. Water it once a week.

4 As the plant grows bigger, replant it into a bigger pot.

5 Plant it in your garden, or ask the landowner's permission to plant in a wood or park.

Find a piece of cardstock and cut it into 6 strips to make 6 plant labels. Write a note to remind yourself what kind of plant or tree you are growing.

I'm a planet hero by growing this.............................................tree!

I'm zapping climate change by growing this..........................tree!

I'm helping the planet by growing this....................................tree!

I'm cleansing our air by growing this....................................tree!

I'm treasuring our Earth by growing this...............................tree!

I'm hugging our planet by growing this....................................tree!

10

Make an endangered tiger face.

# ADOPT A WILD ANIMAL

## to protect its home

Many animals are endangered. People can protect them by adopting them. Ask an adult to help you research how you can help too.

By adopting a tiger, you can help stop its rainforest home from being cut down.

Supporting a polar bear will protect it from being hunted.

# Make an origami tiger face to honor endangered animals

Find a square sheet of red or orange paper to fold into a tiger's face. The paper should be at least 8 x 8 inches (21 cm x 21 cm).

1 Fold the paper in half with the tiger face at the top.

2 Turn over. Fold the left and right corners to the bottom point.

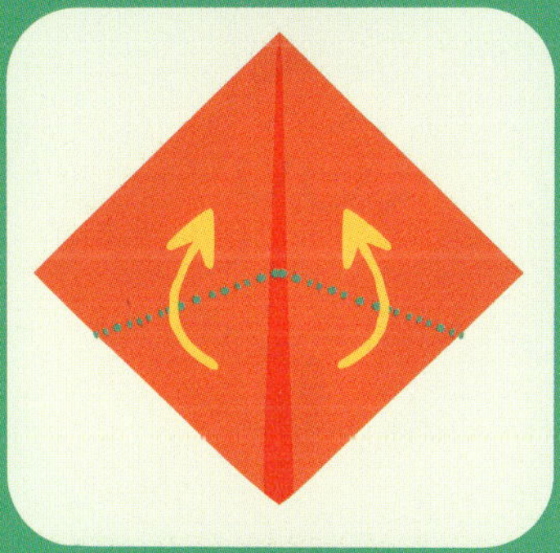

3 Turn up the bottom two flaps to make the ears.

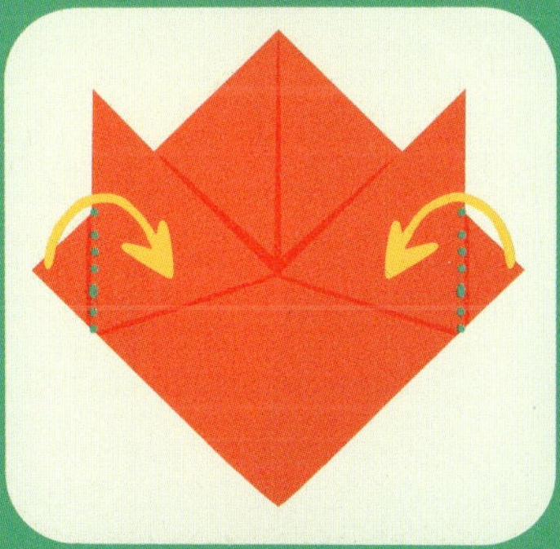

4 Fold in the two flaps at the edge.

5 Turn the paper over so you can see the face.

6 Fold the bottom corner up to cover the nose.

7 Fold a small flap down to create the nose tip.

8 Fold back the triangle at the top behind the head.

9 Decorate the tiger using markers. Display the tiger to remind you to help the animals.

11

Make some trumpets for your friends.

# RECYCLE TRASH

## to make musical instruments

**Don't throw away all your trash. Turn it into something else. Make instruments and form a band!**

Use a couple of old lids to bang as cymbals.

Fill jars or bottles with buttons to make shakers.

Beat tin cans as drums.

### Make jam jar music

1 Keep and wash out your old glass jam jars and bottles.

2 Fill each container with different amounts of water.

3 Tap the jars and bottles with a wooden spoon to create sounds.

4 Make a colorful run of notes by filling each one with a different amount of colored water. Now you can play a tune!

Trace over the templates to make three trumpets.

## Make trumpets for your recycled trash band

1 Trace and cut out the cone shape above. Stick into a cone shape with eco-glue.

2 Create a tube from rolled up card or a toilet paper roll. Snip small tabs along one end.

3 Bend the tabs down on one end.

4 Slot the tube through a cone. Glue in place.

5 Now, hand out your trumpets to your friends and jam!

12

Fold an apple seed tray.

# PLANT AN APPLE TREE

## to help save the bees

Apple trees grow best in a sunny, sheltered place.

Bees are very important. They help to pollinate a third of our crops. But over-building and over-farming mean that there is less land for the flowers that bees need to feed.

It's fun to grow an apple tree from seed. But it will take several years to produce apples.

Bees love apple blossom. They take the sweet nectar and turn it into honey.

## Fold a seed tray to plant apple seeds

Find a square sheet of card in any color you like to make a seed tray. Use the box to plant apple seeds. Add a little soil to the bottom and some seeds. Remember to water!

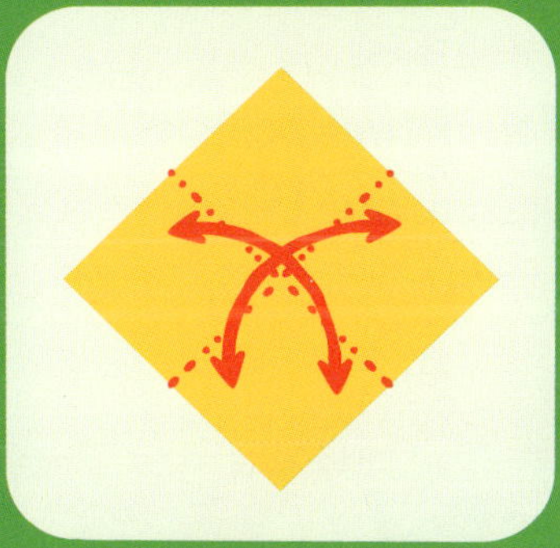

1 Cut a square of paper 8 x 8 inches (21 cm x 21 cm). Fold and unfold.

2 Fold each corner to meet the center until you have a square.

3 Fold the top and bottom sides to the center and unfold.

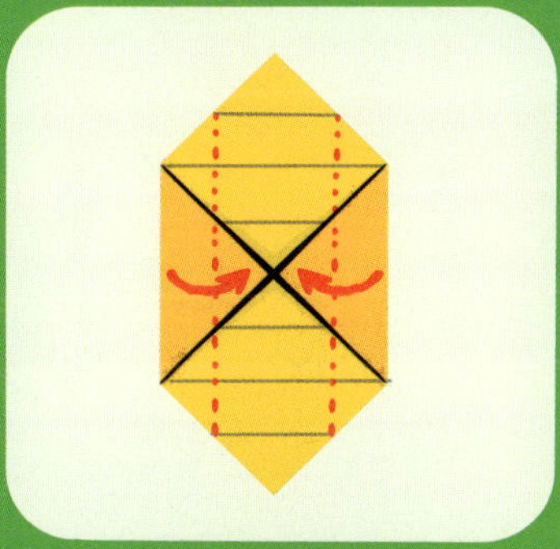

4 Open the top and bottom flaps. Fold the sides in to meet in the center.

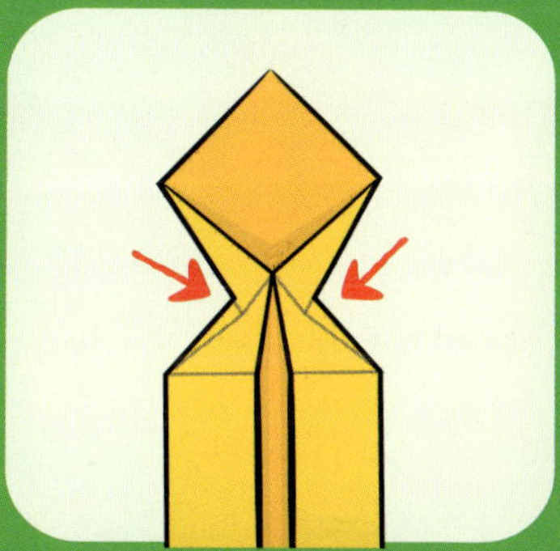

5 Pull both side openings down to pinch the triangles together.

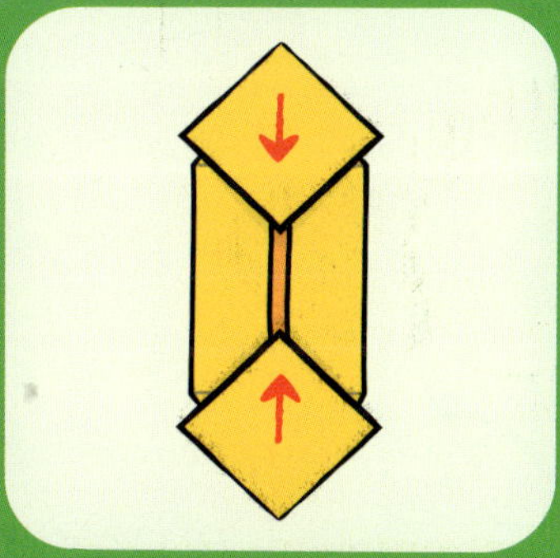

6 Flatten the folds to create the box sides.

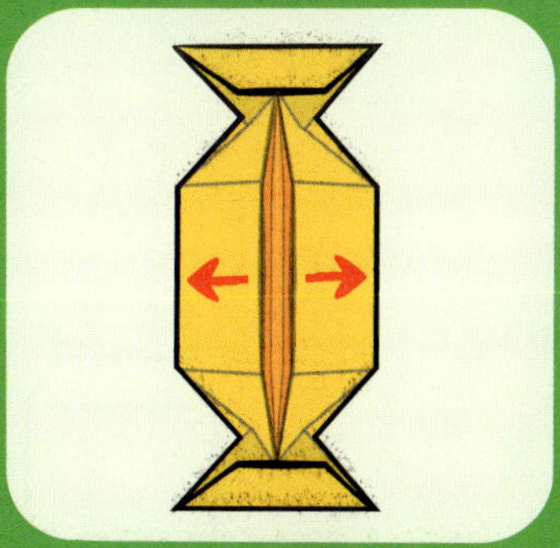

7 Pull the sides up and apart to create the box sides.

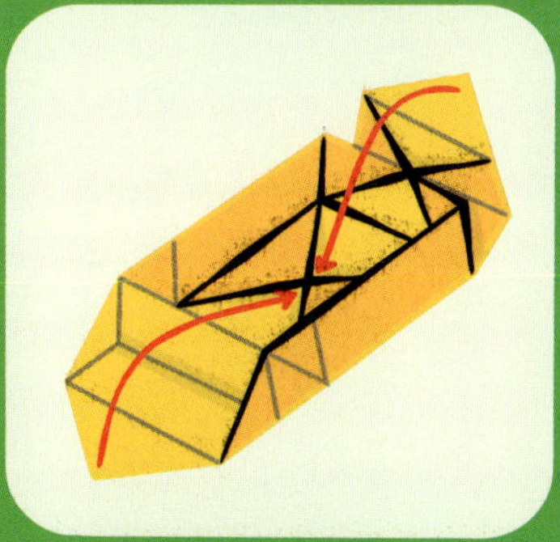

8 Fold one end up and over the side. Tuck the ends in.

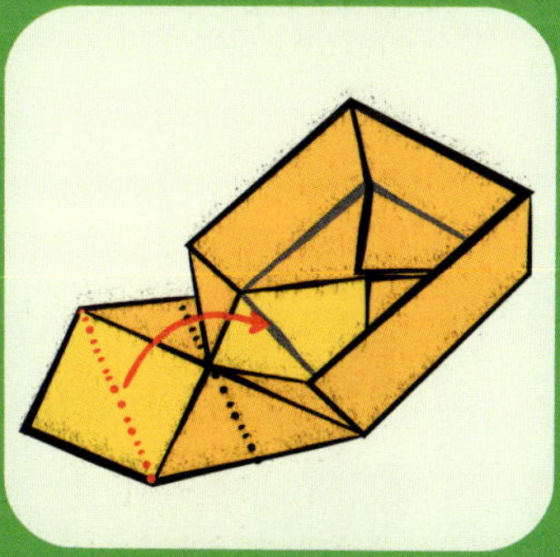

9 Repeat with the other end to complete the box.

13

Send out litter pick invitations.

# HAVE A LITTER PICK

## to clean up our shared spaces

Litter heroes unite! We've only got one home, so let's keep it clean. Host a litter pick, or clean-up, with your friends and family to stop polluting our planet.

Litter contains harmful chemicals that poison the Earth.

Wear protective clothing while picking up litter.

### Invite your friends to a litter pick

1 Choose a park, beach, or road in your area to litter pick.

2 Put on your superhero litter gloves and boots.

3 Give everyone a collection bag to fill with litter.

4 Set your watches! Who can fill their bag first?

5 Sort through the litter to recycle as much as you can.

Invite your friends to a litter pick party!
Copy the invitation shown here
or design your own!

14

Turn over to make reminder notices.

# CHASE AWAY VAMPIRES

## to save electric power in your home

WATCH OUT! There are vampires in your home! Vampires are electrical objects that suck power – even when you think you aren't using them.

HUNT THE RED-EYED MONSTER

One house could save as much as ten percent of its electricity by cutting out the standbys.

Take control of your gadgets (ask an adult to help)

1 If your TV has a red light on, it's using power. Consider unplugging it.

2 Check your games consoles, DVD players and cable boxes too.

3 Turn off your computer and printer. Standby is still sucking.

4 Turn off digital clocks on microwaves and radios. They are still using power.

5 Unplug devices when they are charged. Don't plug them in all night.

Make some reminders to leave around your house. Decorate notices and place them around your house to chase away vampires! Here are some ideas to inspire you.

## Turn me off!

Standby sucks power

## Check the charge!

Turn it off

## Don't be a mug, unplug!

## Goodbye, standby!

Hunt down wasted power

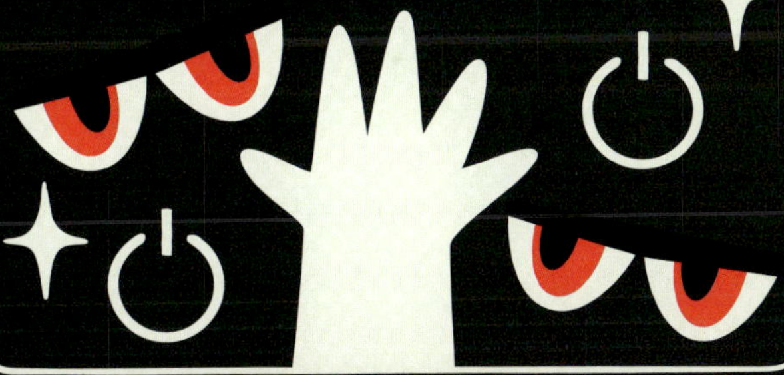

## Don't overcharge!

Save the planet

## Hunt the red-eyed monster

Unplug the TV

# 15

Build a bug hotel with rooms for little critters.

# BUILD A BUG HOTEL

## to protect the mini-recyclers

**Minibeasts help to pollinate flowers, and many recycle dead plants into soil again. Build them a safe home.**

! WARNING!
Do not touch the bug hotel once your guests have arrived. Some creatures can bite or sting.

### You will need

- leaves & grass
- bark
- tin cans
- pine cones
- twigs
- rolled paper tubes
- dried moss

### Make a bug hotel

1 Ask an adult to clean some used cans and make sure that there are no sharp edges.

2 Fill the cans with either bark, twigs, pine cones, leaves, moss or grass.

3 Roll paper tubes for the bees.

4 Stack the cans in a shady spot and wait for your bug hotel guests to arrive!

Cut out some rectangles from cardstock measuring 6 inches x 4 inches (15 cm x 10 cm). You can trace around the rectangle below and copy the designs if you like.

16

Make recycle labels for your bins.

# SORT AND RECYCLE

## to reduce landfill

Ask an adult to repair electrical goods. If they can't, take them to a recycling center.

We don't need to throw everything into a landfill. Recycle as much as you can. Think of ways to separate your trash.

Recycle paper. This saves trees!

Recycle your clothing. Very little of our clothing is recycled when most of it could be!

Compost your food scraps so they break down in a healthy way.

Have separate containers for different types of trash. Make some labels to put on each container.

## PAPER

Save the trees, recycle paper.

## ELECTRICALS

Ask an adult to repair your electricals.

## RAW FOOD SCRAPS

Set up a family compost.

## BATTERIES

Take batteries to a recycling center.

## GLASS

Reuse or recycle all glass.

## CLOTHES

Give away or recycle your old clothes.

17

Fold a seed collection pouch.

# PLANT WILD SEEDS

## to save the butterflies

When land is cleared to grow crops or build homes, flowers are lost. Wildflowers produce the nectar that butterflies drink.

Some butterflies help to pollinate by taking pollen from flower to flower.

Caterpillars and butterflies are important food for birds and small animals.

Find out which flowers attract butterflies and grow them in a pot.

## Create a seed collection pouch

1 Cut out a square of paper. The paper should be at least 8 x 8 inches (20 x 20 cm). Fold it in half.

2 Fold the bottom right corner up to the edge.

3 Repeat with the bottom left corner.

4 Tuck the front top triangle into the pocket.

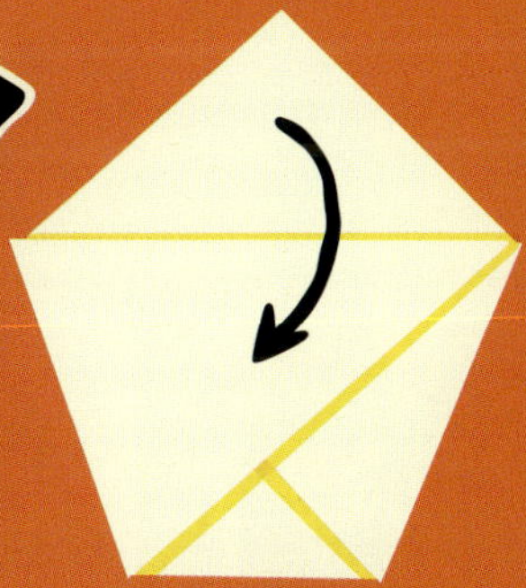

5 Fill your pouch with wildflower seeds and fold the top down.

# 18

Play the I spy game at the bottom of the page.

# BIKE OR HIKE

## instead of using the car

Next time you plan a family day out, leave the car at home! Cars give off harmful fumes that lead to climate change.

Walking and cycling don't harm the planet like cars and buses do.

Try to spot birds and other animals.

Check the weather first and wear the right clothes!

Don't forget to pack a reusable water bottle.

## Play nature I spy on your day out

1 Create alphabet squares by following the instructions on the next page.

2 Get each person on your bike or hike to pick out the same number of squares.

3 Search for the things on your pictures or anything beginning with the letters.

4 First to find them all, or whoever finds the most, is the winner!

5 Save the squares for another game on your next trip.

Divide a piece of paper into squares. Write a letter of the alphabet in each square. Draw pictures of things you might see outdoors on the others. You can copy the squares on this page if you like!

**19** Fold a sweet origami bird.

# FEED THE BIRDS

## to keep our ecosystem healthy

Hang up a pine cone feeder.

Birds help control pests by eating insects.

Birds help carry seeds to faraway places.

Many animals struggle to find food when land is cleared for building or farming. Help feed the birds to keep the wildlife thriving.

### You will need

pine cone

string

food mix of bird seeds, grated cheese, raisins and nuts

peanut butter or lard

! If you have a peanut allergy, use lard instead.

### Make a pine cone feeder

1 Mix the peanut butter or the lard with the food mix until it all holds together.

2 Ask an adult to cut some string. Attach it to the top of the pine cone. Tie a knot.

3 Squash the mixture into the gaps in the pine cone. Hang it up outside for the birds.

## Fold an origami bird

Find a square sheet of paper in any color you like. The paper should be at least 8 x 8 inches (20 x 20 cm).

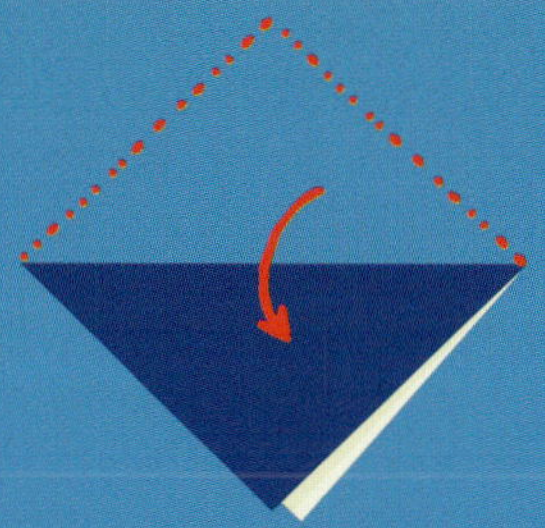

1 Cut out the bird paper. Fold it in half.

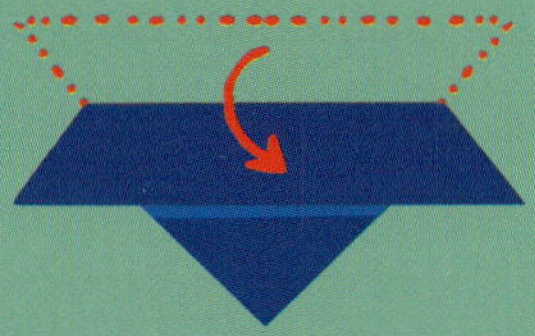

2 Fold the top part of the triangle down.

3 Turn over and fold the top flap up.

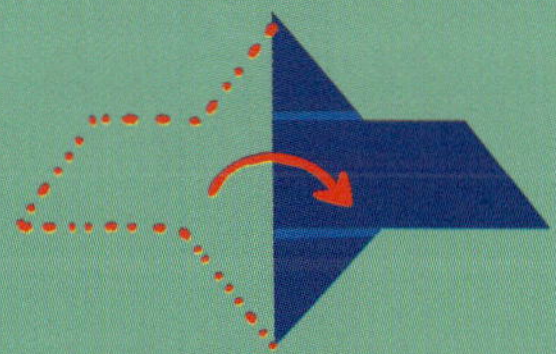

4 Fold the shape in half from left to right.

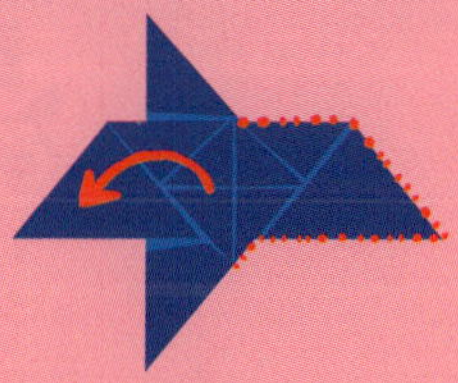

5 Now, fold the right flap back to make a wing.

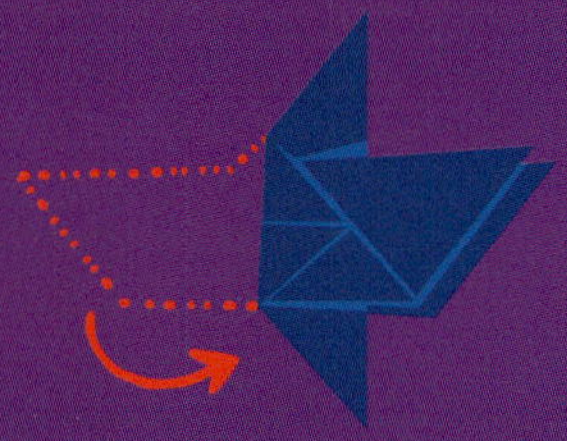

6 Turn over and fold the other wing back.

7 Fold a little triangle over for the beak.

8 Put your bird on display!

**20**

Design a badge for your new outfit.

# SWAP, MIX AND MATCH

## to reuse your clothes

Don't throw away your old clothes. Throw a swap party instead! Mix, match, and swap to stop good clothes from wasting away in a landfill.

Copy the shapes on paper. Color them in and cut them out.

## Wear a mix-and-match badge to encourage everyone to clothes swap

1 Cut some badge shapes about 2 x inches (5 x 7 cm).

2 Ask an adult to poke a safety pin through the top.

3 Cut out your mix of face parts and arrange a crazy face.

4 Use glue to stick the pieces on.

5 Wear your badge to show you're proud to mix and match.

Glue a precious raindrop ornament.

# SAVE WATER

## to make sure we all have enough

Less than one percent of the water on Earth is available to use. The rest is seawater or locked in ice.

Every drop of water we use must be cleaned afterwards. This uses energy and electricity.

A dripping tap can waste a whole bathtub full of water in one day!

Water is precious. We need to drink it to survive, and we use it in our homes and factories. Save water to keep it plentiful.

### How can I save water?

Look after our water by using less. Every drip counts!

1 Turn off the tap while you brush your teeth.

2 Reuse bath water to feed the plants.

3 Take a shorter shower and turn it off while you soap.

4 Reuse a drinking glass all day to save from washing dishes too much.

# Make a raindrop mobile to remind you how precious water is

Trace around this raindrop shape on some pretty paper six times to make the raindrop ornament.

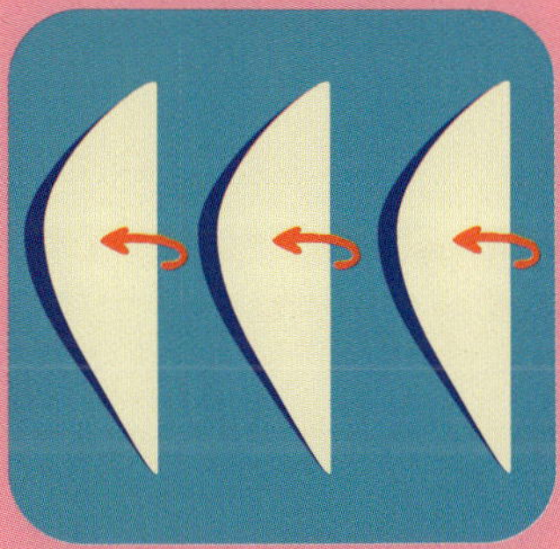

1 Copy the drop shape six times and cut each drop out. Fold each drop in half as shown here.

2 Make some eco-glue (turn to project 30 for the recipe). Glue the back of one drop.

3 Stick another drop on top. Keep gluing and sticking all the drops.

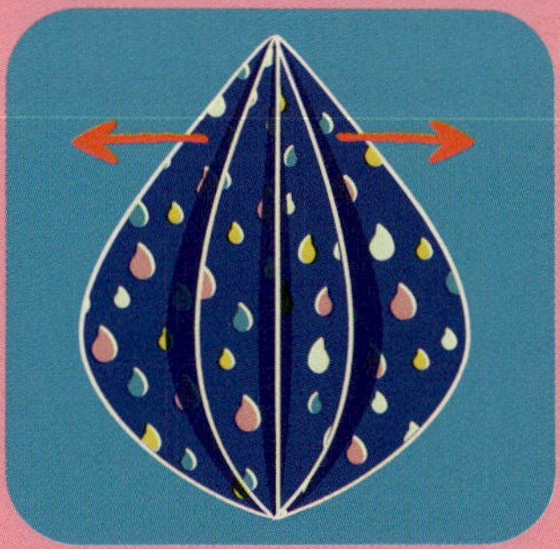

4 Open it up, sticking the last sides together.

5 Sew a piece of thread to the top and hang it up.

22

Make a plastic-free gift bag.

# BUY LESS PLASTIC

## to stop polluting our planet

**One hundred million plastic bottles are sold each day. It can take them 1,000 years to break down. What happens to them?**

## Make a plastic-free gift bag

Decorate a piece of paper about 8 x 8 inches (21 x 21 cm) in size and follow the steps to make a gift bag!

1 Fold over a piece of paper, leaving a strip down the side.

2 Make the eco-glue on the last page. Glue the strip.

3 Fold the strip over so it glues back onto the page. Press it down.

4 Fold a flap up at the bottom, at least 1 inch (3 cm) deep.

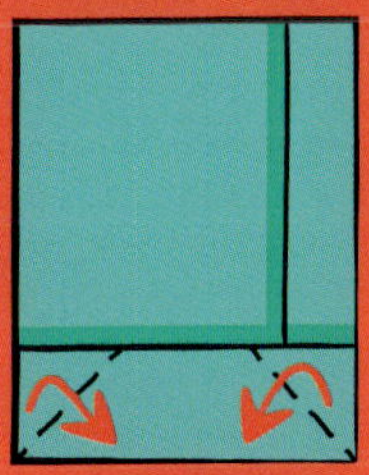

5 Fold down a triangle on each side of the flap.

6 Unfold the triangle corners again.

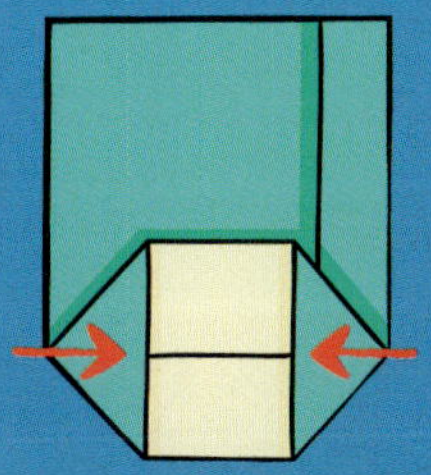

7 Open up the base and tuck the corners inside.

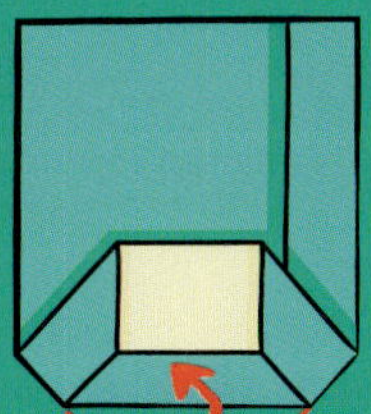

8 Fold up a small flap from the bottom.

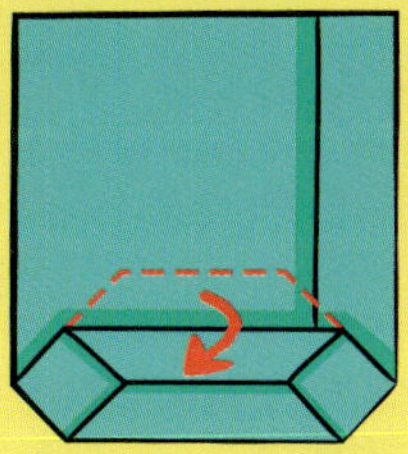

9 Fold the top over and glue it to the bottom flap.

10 Open up the bag and pop in a gift!

**23**

Spread seeds in a garden.

# THROW A SEED BALL

## to rewild a built-up area

When land is cleared to build towns and cities, nature can disappear. Help bring back wildlife by planting wildflowers from seed balls.

### You will need

### Make seed balls

1 Use a spoon to mix together 2 cups of soil and 1/2 cup of flour.

2 Slowly add about 1/2 cup (118 ml) of water to bind it, like dough. Roll it into balls.

3 Roll the balls in a tray filled with seeds that grow naturally in your local area.

4 Throw a seed ball onto a bare patch of earth. With rain and sun, it will grow!

# Make seed paper (ask an adult to help with the blender)

1 Tear some paper into tiny pieces. Soak in water overnight.

2 Mix the paper in a blender with twice as much water as paper.

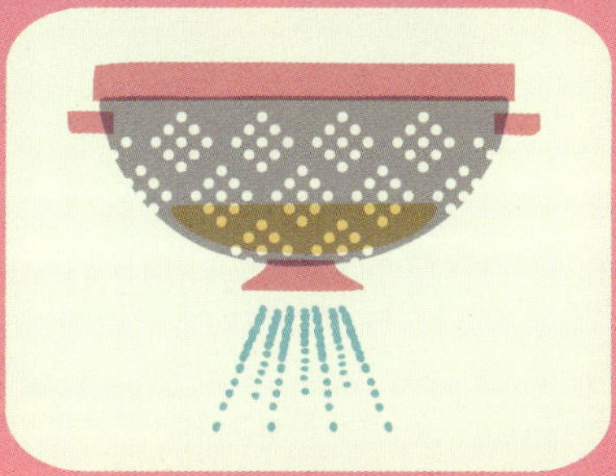

3 Strain the mixture, then squeeze the water out by hand.

4 Flatten onto a cloth-lined tray. Press seeds on top and dry.

5 Write to a friend. Ask them to bury the paper to grow the seeds!

24

Play the energy hero game.

# MAKE A DIFFERENCE

## in your own home

You can save energy all day, every day! Each bit you save will help to reduce climate change.

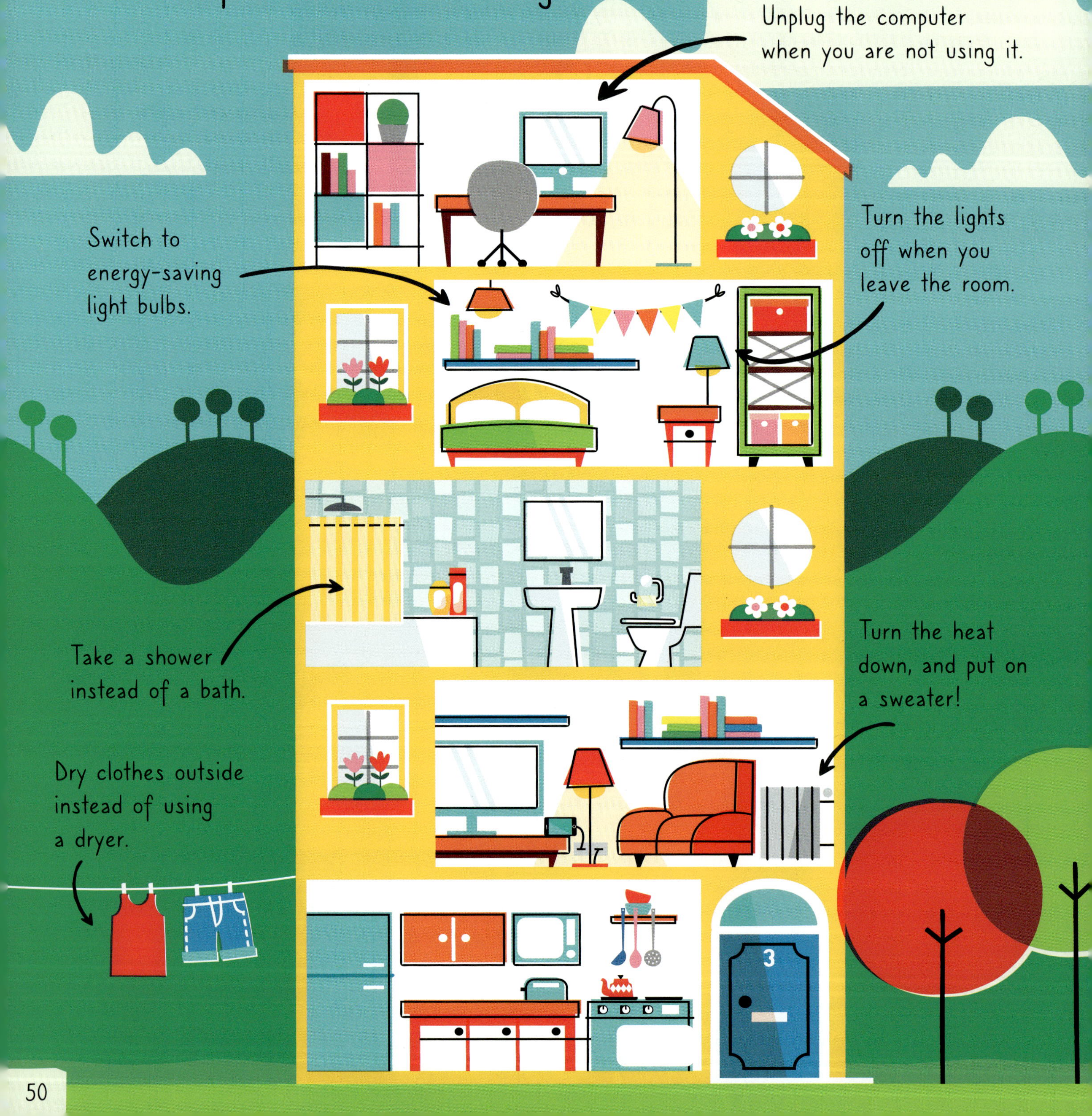

## Play the energy hero game

1. Copy the challenges below and put them in a jar.
2. Ask everyone in your household to pick out one challenge.
3. Everyone must keep the challenge up for one week.
4. At the end of the week, award each person points.
5. Whoever has the most points is the energy hero!
6. Pick again next week. Who is the hero this time?

**HEATING INSPECTOR** Monitor the heating or air conditioning morning, noon, and night. Can you turn it down or off?

**COMPUTER MANAGER** Check throughout the day that any computer that is not in use is fully turned off.

**SHOWER DETECTIVE** At least once a week ask everyone to take a short shower instead of a bath.

**PHONE SLEUTH** Unplug all phones and devices when they are fully charged.

**FUN DIRECTOR** Encourage the family to play games that don't use any electricity!

**TOOTHBRUSH BOSS** Take a peek to check that each person has turned the tap off while brushing their teeth.

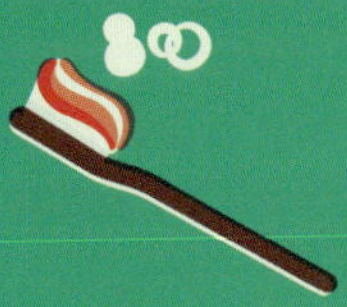

**LIGHT MONITOR** Check that all lights are off when no one is in a room.

**WASHING CHIEF** Keep the washing machine temperature at no higher than 86°F (30°C), unless clothes are really dirty.

**25**

Make a rug loom to weave fabric scraps.

# RESCUE OLD CLOTHES

## to reuse the fabric

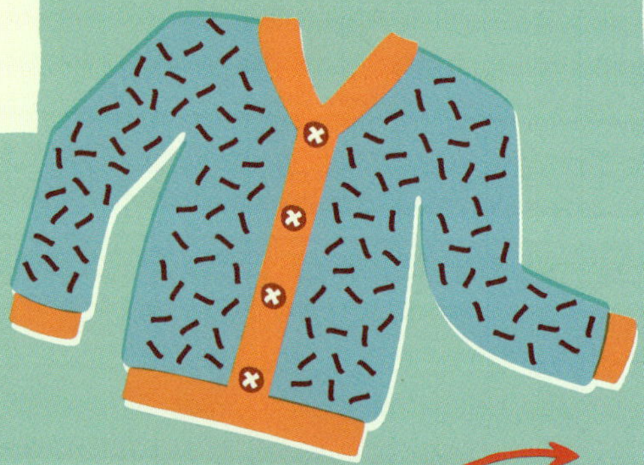

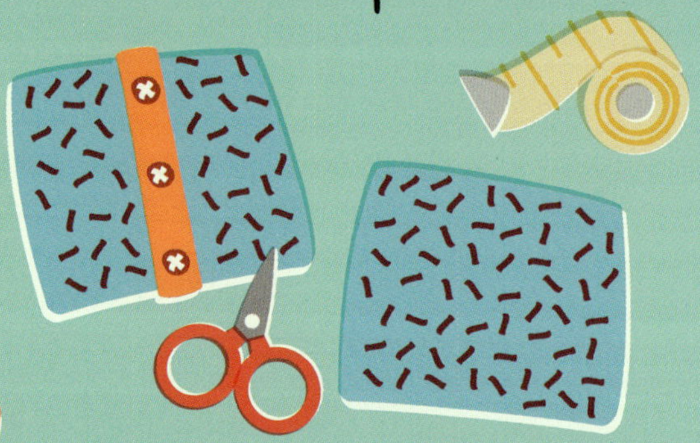

1 Don't throw away your old button-up cardigan or top!

2 With an adult, cut the front and back into two squares the same size.

3 Pin the squares together with the fronts inside and the buttons done up.

**If you can't mend or reuse clothes, fashion them into something completely new!**

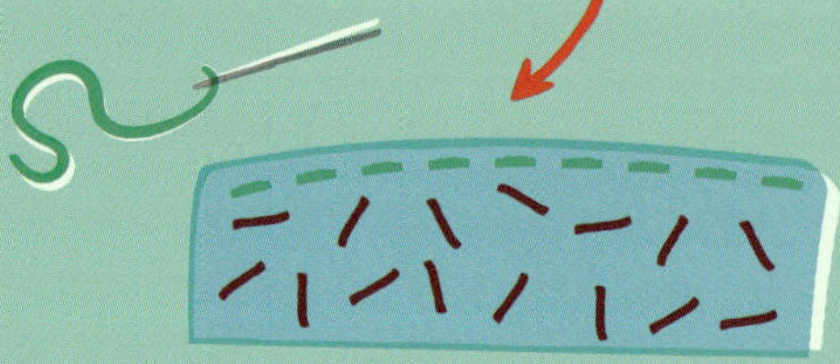

4 Sew the edges together with a thick thread or wool.

5 Open the buttons and turn the cushion inside out.

6 Stuff the cushion with other old clothes and close the buttons.

### Turn your worn-out clothes into a rag rug by making a loom!

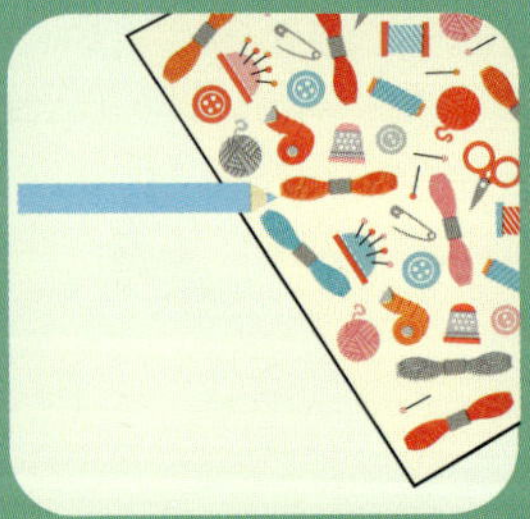

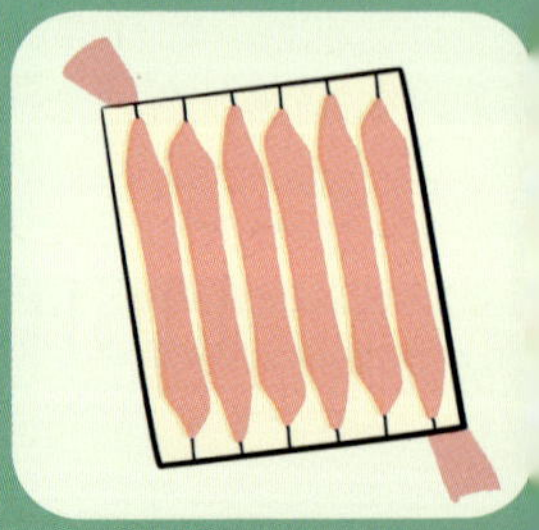

1 Cut a square of cardboard 8 x 8 inches (20 x 20 cm). Draw a design on one side of it.

2 Mark every 0.5 inch (1.2 cm) along the top and bottom. Snip a 1 inch (2.5 cm) line down every mark.

3 Ask an adult to help you cut up old scraps of fabric into 1-inch- (1.2 cm) wide strips.

4 Knot the strips together into one long strip.

5 Thread the strip through each slit, from top to bottom, front to back.

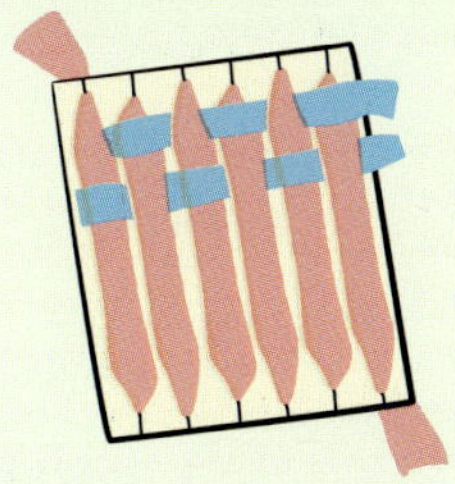

6 Weave a different strip of fabric from side to side, under and over.

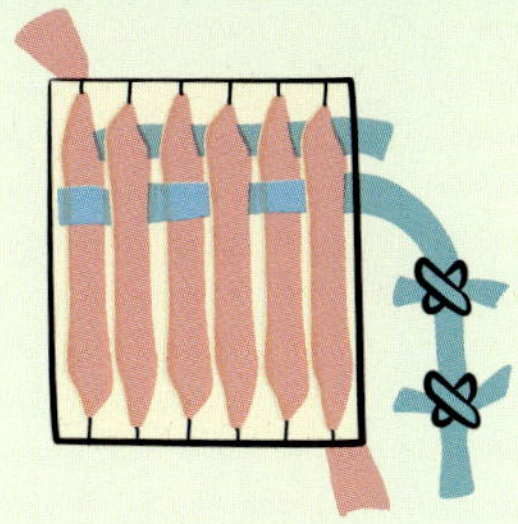

7 Keep weaving. Knot on new strips as they run out.

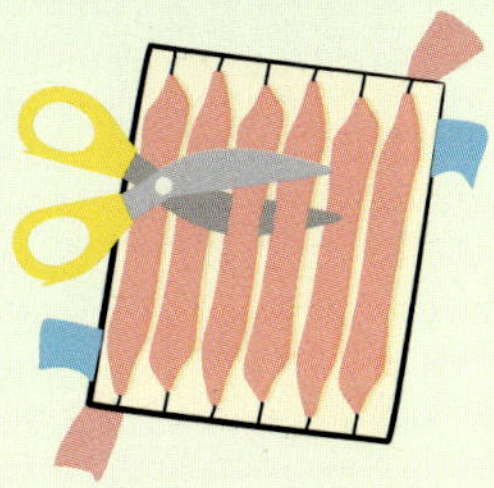

8 When you've finished, turn it over. Cut the strips across the back.

9 Remove the frame. Knot together the loose pairs of strips.

10 If there are any straggly ends, trim them to neaten.

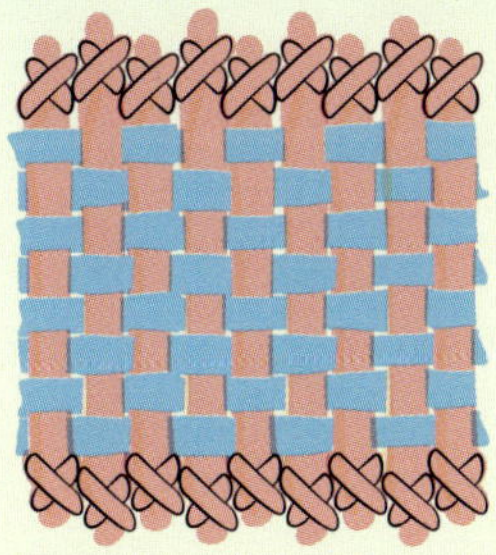

11 Use it as a place mat, or sew lots together for a rug!

Use this as inspiration for your loom design..

# 26

Bake an eco-friendly pizza.

# MAKE YOUR OWN PIZZA

## without chemicals or food miles

Cook an eco-friendly pizza from scratch. That way, you save food miles, go organic, and it tastes great too!

Share your eco-pizza with a friend.

Go organic by growing fruit and vegetables without chemical pesticides.

### You will need

- 2 large pots
- garden stake
- tomato plant
- onion, pepper, basil, chives, thyme, and oregano seeds
- compost

### Grow your own pizza sauce

1 Repot the tomato plant into a large container. Add a stake for it to grow up.

2 Plant the seeds. Put your pots in a sunny spot and water regularly.

3 If possible, introduce a ladybug. It will eat the pests that eat the plants!

4 After 6-8 weeks, harvest the fully grown plants to make pizza sauce.

# Bake an organic pizza

Use your homegrown harvest to make fresh pizza sauce! If you can, buy organic, locally made bread and cheese too. Ask an adult to help you to follow the steps below.

## Ingredients

- 2 peppers
- 1 onion
- 1/2 cup of chopped basil, chives, thyme, and oregano
- cheese
- 1 small baguette
- 2 teaspoon oil
- 8-10 tomatoes

1 Ask for help chopping the onions, peppers, and tomatoes into chunks.

2 Ask for help grating enough cheese to fill 1/2 cup. Preheat the oven to 400°F (200°C).

3 Ask an adult to help you heat the oil and onion in a pan. Cook for two minutes on medium heat.

4 Add the tomatoes, peppers, and herbs to the pan and stir on medium heat for 12-15 minutes.

5 Ask for help cutting the baguette in half. Spread the sauce on and sprinkle lots of cheese on top.

6 Put the baguette into the oven for 10 minutes, or until the cheese melts. Ask an adult to help you take it out.

27

Make the eco flip-flapper game.

# AVOID PLASTIC

## to stop harming our animals

**Plastic can smell, taste, or even look like food to animals. When they eat it, plastic can be deadly.**

Popped balloons have ended up in the bellies of kangaroos.

Elephants and other animals sometimes eat plastic waste.

Squirrels, and other small animals, get their heads stuck in tubs, trying to reach food.

Look after your pets. Sharp plastic can cut their paws.

### Try the flip-flapper eco-quiz

1 Copy and fold the flip-flapper on the next page. Ask a friend to pick a number.

2 Push open and pull apart the flip-flapper as many times as the number chosen.

3 Ask your friend to choose an animal that they can see.

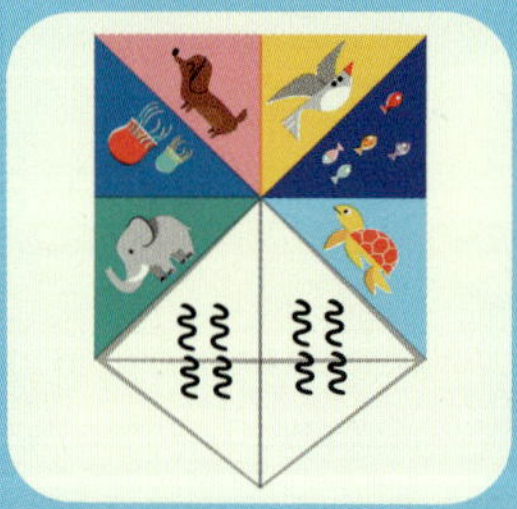

4 Open up the flip-flapper under the animal to find the question and answer.

5 If they answer correctly, they can have another turn. If not, it's your turn.

1 2 3 4 5 6 7 8

**Name three land animals that are harmed by plastic.**

Example answers: Elephants, seabirds, bears, kangaroos, squirrels, badgers, dogs and other pets.

**How long does it take plastic to break down?**

Answer: It can take up to 1,000 years.

**Name three ways you can use less plastic.**

Example answers: Avoid using plastic bottles, straws, bags, and toothbrushes. Avoid buying food in plastic packaging.

**Can you think of two ocean creatures that are harmed by plastic?**

Example answers: Turtles, seals, whales, dolphins, penguins, fish, or crabs.

**What can you use instead of a plastic toothbrush?**

Answer: A bamboo toothbrush, which is natural and breaks down easily.

**How do you pack a plastic-free picnic?**

Answer: Buy no food with plastic packaging. Pack the food into reusable containers and use reusable bottles, plates, and cutlery.

**What can you use instead of a plastic shopping bag?**

Example answers: Use a canvas, paper, or cotton bag that you can either use again or recycle.

**Is it OK to use plastic straws?**

Answer: No. Plastic straws are used once, then thrown away. Every day millions are used – that's a lot of plastic pollution.

## Make a flip-flapper

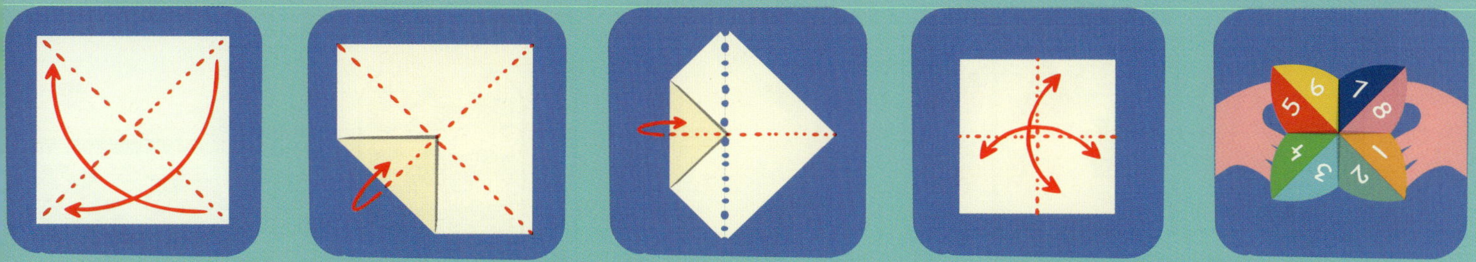

1. Copy the page above onto a square of paper 8 x 8 inches (20 x 20 cm).
2. Fold all four corners to the center so they reach the middle.
3. Turn over and fold each corner to the center again.
4. Fold in half both ways and unfold to loosen the flaps.
5. Tuck a finger and thumb beneath each flap to play the game!

28

Learn to use up all your food.

# EAT UP
## to stop food waste

A third of the world's food is thrown away. Food waste in landfills releases poisonous gases that heat up the air, increasing climate change.

It takes a lot of energy, water and farmland to produce food.

Many people don't have enough food, so don't waste it!

### Waste less food in your home

1 Try not to buy, cook, or put on your plate more food than you really need.

2 Buy less food by growing your own. There will be less plastic packaging too.

3 Don't throw away your odd-shaped vegetables. They taste just as good.

4 Compost vegetable and fruit peelings instead of putting them in the trash.

5 Don't throw away food unless it has gone bad.

# French toast

## Ingredients

2 slices of bread. They can be a bit stale, but not moldy.

1 teaspoon oil

1/2 teaspoon cinnamon

1 teaspoon vanilla extract

1 egg

1/4 cup milk

1 Crack the egg into a bowl and whisk it to mix it up.

2 Pour in the milk, cinnamon, and vanilla, and whisk until it is all mixed in.

3 Dip the bread into the mixture. Make sure both sides are covered.

4 Ask an adult to help pour the oil into a pan and fry the bread on both sides until golden.

# Ripe banana pancakes

## Ingredients

1/2 cup natural yogurt

1 tablespoon oil

1 egg

1 ripe banana

1 tablespoon honey

syrup

1 cup oats

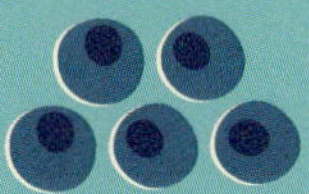

a handful of blueberries

1 Put the yogurt, banana, oats, egg, and honey into a blender and blitz.

2 Ask an adult to heat a little oil in a pan and pour in some of the batter.

3 When the pancake begins to bubble, ask an adult to flip it. Fry until golden brown.

4 Serve with a drizzle of syrup, blueberries, and a few banana slices.

29

Make eco-badges to wear and to share.

# SPREAD THE WORD

## to help save the planet

Everyone needs to help when it comes to saving the planet. But even little actions can make a BIG difference. Shout loudly and get everyone involved!

### Make badges to pass on your message

1 Draw around a jam jar lid several times on some paper. Cut out the circles.

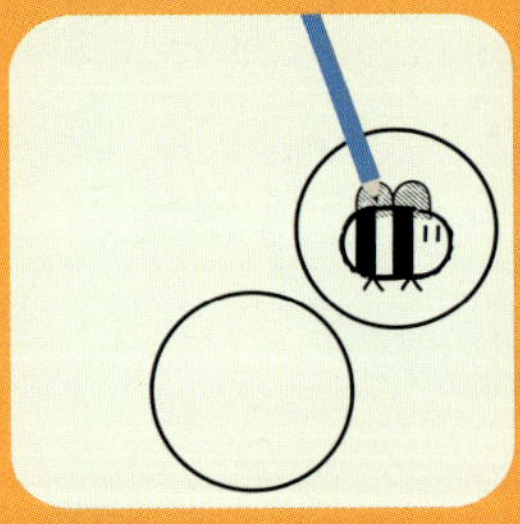

2 Copy the pictures on the next page and color them in.

3 Glue the pictures onto some sturdy paper with eco-glue (project 30).

4 Fasten a safety pin to the back with eco-friendly tape.

5 Wear your badge with pride or give it to a friend!

Save the bees!
Recycle me
Adopt a tiger
Bring back wildflowers
Save our oceans!
Go green
Go cycling
Save energy
Be a litter hero!
Save water
Recycle, recycle,
recycle
Save our trees
Say no to plastic!
Help bees, plant seeds
Stop food waste!
Make compost, not landfill
Make friends with a bug
Go organic
Adopt a polar bear
Cut plastic, save ocean creatures
Go green, grow your own
Plant a tree
Save the Earth

30

Make natural glue to use in your projects.

# MAKE ECO-FRIENDLY GLUE

Try making this eco-friendly glue for your projects. Other glues have harmful chemicals in them and are also stored in plastic containers. This glue is easy to make, completely natural, and it works well too!

WARNING! Ask an adult to help you to make the glue.

**You will need**

3 tablespoons flour

1 tablespoon of sugar

Some cold water

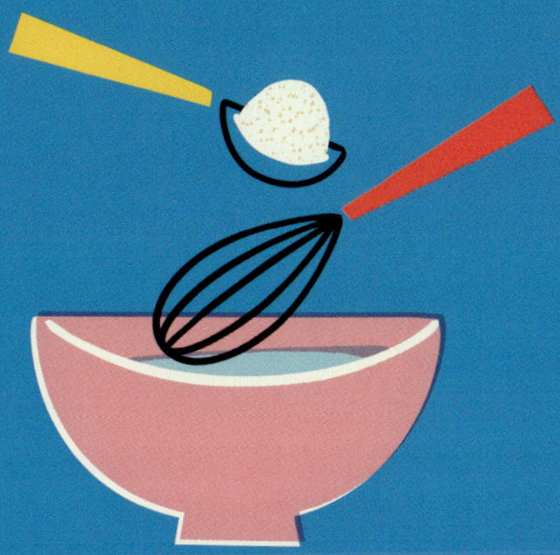

1 Mix the flour with 4 tablespoons of cold water in a bowl. Whisk it until it's smooth.

2 Pour a cup of water into a pan. Ask an adult to turn on the heat. Wait until it boils.

3 Slowly add the flour paste to the boiling water. Mix with a wooden spoon until it thickens.

4 When the mixture has thickened, turn off the heat. Stir in the sugar.

5 Leave the mixture to cool, then pour it into a jar.

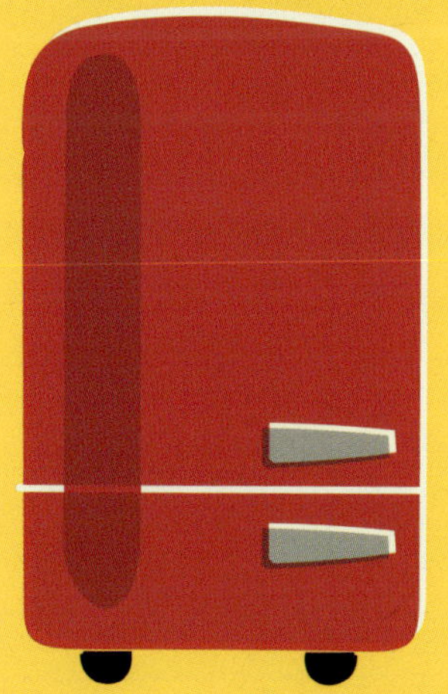

6 Keep the eco-glue in the fridge. It will last for up to two weeks.

Published in 2026 by Windmill Books,
an Imprint of Rosen Publishing
2544 Clinton St.
Buffalo, NY 14224



Written by Susan Hayes and Penny Arlon
Illustrated by Pintachan
Consultancy by Dr Amy Dickman

Many thanks to eco-warrior project-makers Meg and Sylvie

Cataloging-in-Publication Data
Names: Hayes, Susan, author. | Arlon, Penelope, author. | Pintachan, illustrator.
Title: The book of eco paper projects / by Susan Hayes and Penelope Arlon, illustrated by Pintachan.
Description: Buffalo, NY : Windmill Books, 2026. | Series: The extraordinary activity library
Identifiers: ISBN 9781725396647 (pbk.) | ISBN 9781725396654 (library bound) | ISBN 9781725396661 (ebook)
Subjects: LCSH: Sustainable living--Juvenile literature. | Biodegradable products--Juvenile literature. | Recycling (Waste, etc.)--Juvenile literature. | Environmental responsibility--Juvenile literature.
Classification: LCC GE195.5 H39 2026 | DDC 363.7--dc23



Adult supervision is advised for eco-activities within the book.
Always ask an adult for help when using glue, paint and scissors.
Wear protective clothing and cover surfaces to avoid staining.

Printed in the United States of America

CPSIA Compliance Information: Batch #CSWM26
For Further Information contact Rosen Publishing at 1-800-237-9932